The Wisdom Codex: Stoic, Eastern, And Historical Wisdom To Think Better And Live Deeper

Harry Jozef

Table of contents

Introduction — Why a "Wisdom Codex" Now?

"We suffer more in imagination than in reality." Seneca wrote that nearly two thousand years ago, yet it reads like a line pulled from your last anxious afternoon. You replay a conversation that hasn't happened yet. You catastrophize a decision that could go five different ways, most of them fine. You feel the body tighten before the facts even arrive. The pain is real, but its source is often a story the mind tells too fast and too convincingly. This book begins there, not to shame the mind for doing what minds do, but to train it to do better. If suffering grows in imagination, then relief can grow in clarity. That is the wager of a Wisdom Codex.

You are living in a moment that rewards speed and volume, not judgment. Advice is abundant; discernment is scarce. You can scroll a thousand opinions in ten minutes and still feel unsure what to do next. You can consume motivation daily and feel strangely less motivated. The problem is not a lack of information. It's the absence of a stable way to think, decide, and act when conditions are noisy. A codex is not a manifesto or a mood. It is a working manual. Historically, codices were created to make essential knowledge portable and durable. This one is built for the same reason: to carry with you a small set of principles that hold under pressure, across cultures, and through time.

What this book is, at its core, is a cross-cultural field guide to clearer thinking, steadier emotions, and deeper living. It draws from Stoic practice because it teaches you how to meet events without collapsing or hardening. It draws from Eastern insight because it shows you how to loosen your grip on the self-story that fuels unnecessary suffering. It draws from historical lessons because history is a laboratory that has already run the experiments you are about to run—ambition, fear, power, loss, uncertainty—and recorded the outcomes. None of these streams are treated as relics. They are tools. The aim is not to sound wise but to help you act wisely on an ordinary Tuesday.

Clarity here does not mean becoming emotionless or detached from life. It means learning to see what is happening without adding distortion. When your thinking is clearer, your emotions become informative rather than overwhelming. You can feel anger without letting it drive. You can feel fear without obeying it. You can feel desire without being dragged by it. This steadiness is not numbness; it is reliability. You become someone who can be counted on—by others and by yourself—because your inner weather no longer dictates every move.

Deeper living, in this sense, is not about intensity or constant meaning-making. It is about alignment. Your days line up with what you say matters. Your decisions cost less regret. You recover faster from mistakes because you understand the system you are operating within. You do fewer things, better, with less friction. Depth shows up as quiet confidence: the sense that even when you don't know what will happen, you know how you will respond.

Just as important is what this book is not. It is not a quote collection designed to make you feel briefly inspired and then oddly empty. Quotes can open doors, but they cannot walk you through the room. It is not vague encouragement that tells you everything will work out if you just believe hard enough. Belief without method collapses under stress. Each chapter in this codex takes ideas that have survived centuries and turns them into decisions you can make, habits you can build, and mental models you can use today. If an idea cannot be translated into action, it does not belong here.

You will not be asked to adopt a new identity or to overhaul your life in a weekend. You will be asked to notice where your attention goes, how you interpret events, and which responses you practice repeatedly. The changes are small by design. They compound. Wisdom is not a personality trait; it is a set of trained responses. The point is not to agree with everything you read, but to test it against your life and keep what works.

Using this codex is intentionally simple. You can read straight through if you want a complete framework, because the chapters build on one another in a deliberate sequence. You will start with how perception shapes experience, move into how emotion follows judgment, and then into how values guide action when outcomes are uncertain. Read this way if you want a map—a sense of how the pieces fit together into a coherent practice.

You can also jump directly to the chapter that matches your current struggle. If fear is loud right now, begin there. If anger is costing you relationships, start with the chapter that teaches you how to pause without suppressing. If uncertainty is freezing you, there is a chapter on decision-making when information is incomplete. If indecision is the pattern, you'll learn how to set criteria that end endless weighing. If meaning feels thin or borrowed, there is guidance for rebuilding it from lived commitments rather than borrowed slogans. This book respects the fact that life rarely presents challenges in a neat order.

At the end of each chapter, you will keep what this codex calls a Commonplace Page. This is an old practice with a modern purpose. You write three lines only. The first is the Principle: a sentence that captures the idea in your own words. Not copied. Owned. The second is the Practice: one small action you will repeat this week that expresses the principle. Something observable. The third is the Proof: a brief note from your own life that shows the practice working, even slightly. Proof is not perfection. It is evidence that you are training, not consuming.

This page matters more than the chapter itself. Writing forces precision. Precision forces commitment. When you come back weeks later, you won't remember every explanation, but you will remember what you practiced and what it changed. Over time, these pages become a personal record of wisdom earned rather than admired from afar.

Treat wisdom here as training, not information. Information lives in the explanations. Training lives in repetition. You do not read about steadiness and become steady. You practice responding differently when the familiar trigger appears. You do not understand impermanence and stop clinging. You rehearse letting go in small, safe moments until the skill is there when it matters. Repetition belongs in practice, not in the prose. If something feels obvious, that is often a sign it deserves practice, not dismissal.

You may notice resistance as you go. Part of you will want novelty, not repetition. Part of you will want certainty, not judgment. Part of you will want to fix others before adjusting yourself. This is normal. The codex does not ask you to defeat these tendencies; it asks you to work with them. You will learn how to place friction where it helps and remove it where it harms.

You will learn how to design your environment and your self-talk so that the better response is easier to choose.

This approach blends traditions without flattening them. Stoic practice offers a clear distinction between what you can influence and what you cannot, and the discipline to invest energy accordingly. Eastern insight reminds you that the self you defend so fiercely is more fluid than it appears, and that relief often comes from loosening, not winning. History shows you the consequences of unchecked pride, fear-driven cruelty, and patient restraint. Together, they form a practical compass. Not north-star inspiration, but bearings you can check when you're lost.

If you are skeptical, that is welcome here. Skepticism sharpens tools. Use it to test, not to avoid. Try the practices. Keep the Commonplace Page. Watch what changes in the next conversation, the next delay, the next disappointment. Wisdom that cannot survive contact with life is decoration. Wisdom that does survive becomes character.

This codex is meant to be lived with. Dog-ear pages. Write in the margins. Argue with a paragraph and then try the exercise anyway. Return to chapters as seasons change. You are not behind if you move slowly. You are training something that lasts.

If you are ready to begin, turn to Chapter 1. You will start where all lasting change starts: with how you see what happens to you, and how that seeing quietly shapes everything that follows.

Chapter 1 — The Inner Citadel: What You Control, What Controls You

“You have power over your mind—not outside events.” — Marcus Aurelius

1.1 The Two Domains: Agency vs. Weather

Picture a stone citadel on a hill. Thick walls. A gate you can open and close. Inside, order. Outside, whatever the world brings—sun, wind, siege, silence. The Stoics used this image to describe the only fortress that truly holds: your inner domain. Not because it keeps life out, but because it gives you a place to stand when life presses in. The problem most people face is not that the world is harsh. It’s that they keep trying to control the weather instead of governing the city.

Begin with a simple distinction that changes everything once you practice it. There are two domains in your life. One is agency: what you can choose directly. The other is weather: what arrives, shifts, and leaves largely on its own schedule. Suffering multiplies when these two are confused. Relief begins when they are separated and treated accordingly.

To build a control map, you don’t need a notebook full of categories. You need honesty. Look at your last week and name three things you can choose in any situation. You can choose your actions. You can choose where your attention rests. You can choose how you interpret what happens before you respond. These are not slogans; they are levers. You decide whether you speak now or later, whether you scroll or breathe, whether you interpret a delay as an insult or as neutral friction. These choices are small, but they are yours.

Now look at what you can only influence, not command. Outcomes live here. Other people's moods live here. Timing lives here. Health trajectories, market shifts, traffic, weather, and reputation live here. You can nudge some of these with effort and skill, but you cannot guarantee them. When you treat influence as control, you invite frustration. When you treat influence as influence, you invest wisely without demanding certainty.

This map matters because energy follows expectation. If you expect control where you have none, you will burn energy arguing with reality. If you underestimate control where you do have it, you will feel helpless even when options exist. The practice is not to shrink your ambition, but to place it precisely.

Consider a familiar example: a difficult conversation. You can choose to prepare, to listen, to speak clearly, to set boundaries. You cannot choose how the other person receives your words, whether they change, or whether they like you afterward. If you aim for approval, you hand the steering wheel to weather. If you aim for integrity of action—say what needs to be said with care—you stay in agency. The outcome may still sting, but it will not corrode you.

Eastern traditions add a crucial refinement here. They notice that much of what we think is "outside" is actually internal weather we've mistaken for fact. A surge of anger feels like a command. A spike of fear feels like a prophecy. The practice is to observe these states without letting them draft policy. You don't deny the cloud; you don't confuse it with the sky. When emotion is treated as weather, it informs without ruling.

The "weather mindset" is not passive acceptance. It is intelligent preparation. You stop negotiating with reality as if it might change its mind if you argue well enough. You prepare for what is likely, you build margins for what is possible, and you move within conditions as they are. Sailors do not curse the wind; they set the sail. Farmers do not demand rain; they plan seasons. Leaders do not wait for perfect conditions; they decide under imperfect ones.

Notice how often stress comes from questions that imply control you don't have. "Why is this happening?" sounds reasonable, but it often hides a protest: this should not be. The mind hunts for causes not to learn, but to reverse reality. Replace that question with one that returns you to agency: "What is this asking of me?" The moment you ask it, your posture changes. You move from complaint to response. From rumination to design.

"What is this asking of me?" might ask for patience in a delay, courage in a confrontation, humility in a correction, or restraint in a victory. It might ask you to rest, to focus, or to let go of a plan that no longer fits. The answer will not always be comfortable, but it will be actionable. And action dissolves anxiety far better than explanation.

History offers endless proof of this distinction. Those who survived long campaigns—political, military, personal—were not the ones who demanded favorable conditions. They were the ones who conserved agency and spent it well. They controlled discipline, morale, and timing when possible, and adapted when not. Those who collapsed often did so not from lack of talent, but from insisting on control over what could not be commanded.

Apply this today in a small way. Choose one recurring irritation. Traffic. Email. A colleague. A family pattern. Draw the control map in your head. Name what is agency here and what is weather. Then act decisively in the agency domain and release the rest. Release does not mean apathy; it means you stop feeding the loop with outrage. You'll feel the difference immediately: a drop in tension, a clearer next step.

There is a subtle trap to avoid. Some people use the idea of control to shrink their life. They say, "I only control my mind," and retreat from effort. That is not the teaching. You control your actions, which shape the field of influence. You show up prepared. You train skills. You make requests. You take risks. You simply refuse to hinge your worth or peace on outcomes you cannot guarantee.

The inner citadel is not isolation. It is stability. From stability, you engage more fully because you are not bargaining for emotional safety with every result. You can be ambitious without being brittle. You can care deeply without clinging.

As you practice this distinction, you will notice a new kind of confidence. Not bravado. Reliability. You know what you will do when plans change. You know where to invest attention when noise rises. You know which questions to ask when the old ones start spinning. This is not optimism; it is competence at living.

Return to the map often. Especially when emotions run high. Especially when outcomes matter. Especially when the mind insists that if you could just think harder, you could force reality to comply. Smile at that impulse. Then set the sail.

In the next section, you will take this foundation and learn how to guard attention itself—the gate of the citadel—so that fewer storms get inside in the first place, and those that do pass through without damage.

1.2 The Trifecta of Control: Attention, Interpretation, Response

If the inner citadel has a gate, attention is it. Whatever you allow through attention determines the tone of your inner life. Under stress, attention tends to scatter or fixate. It jumps to threat, to insult, to what might go wrong next. This is not a moral failure; it's a nervous system doing its job too loudly. Training attention means you stop letting urgency decide what deserves focus.

Begin by noticing where your mind goes when pressure hits. Not in theory, but in the next real moment. Maybe it loops on a message you haven't received. Maybe it scans faces for disapproval. Maybe it rehearses arguments or replays mistakes. The training starts with noticing without commentary. "This is where my attention went." That sentence alone creates space. You are no longer fused with the content; you are observing the movement.

Redirection is the next step, and it must be specific. Vague commands like "calm down" don't work. Choose a simple anchor you can return to on purpose. Your breath for ten seconds. The physical sensation of your feet on the floor. The single task in front of you, done cleanly. Attention grows stronger the same way muscles do: brief, repeated reps under manageable load. Each return counts.

Eastern practices emphasize that attention is not owned by thoughts; it can be trained to rest. Stoic practice adds that where attention rests, judgment follows. When attention is hijacked, interpretation is distorted. So you learn to slow the sequence. Attention first. Then interpretation. Then response.

Interpretation is the story you tell yourself about what you notice. It is fast, convincing, and often invisible. Under stress, it tends to personalize and catastrophize. A delayed reply becomes disrespect. A raised eyebrow becomes rejection. A mistake becomes a verdict on your worth. The skill here is not to eliminate interpretation—that's impossible—but to name it.

Use a simple phrase: "I'm telling myself a story that…" This sentence is disarming. It doesn't argue with the story; it reveals it as a story. "I'm telling myself a story that they don't care." "I'm telling myself a story that this will fail." Once named, the story loosens its grip. You can test it. You can offer alternatives. You can hold it lightly instead of obeying it.

Naming interpretation also protects relationships. Instead of accusing—"You ignored me"—you describe your inner process—"I'm telling myself a story that I was ignored." This invites clarity rather than conflict. It keeps you in agency while opening space for information you don't yet have.

Response is where values show up. Mood pushes for immediacy; values ask for alignment. When tired or threatened, mood wants relief now—snap back, withdraw, indulge, prove. Values want something steadier—honesty, patience, courage, respect. Choosing response means you let values overrule mood, not once heroically, but often quietly.

A practical test helps: ask which response you would respect yourself for tomorrow. Not which feels best now. This shifts the time horizon just enough to cool impulse. You are not suppressing emotion; you are choosing direction. The response can still be firm. It can still set boundaries. It just won't be reactive.

Train this trifecta in low-stakes moments. When the line is long. When the app glitches. When the comment stings a little. Attention: notice the pull. Interpretation: name the story. Response: choose the action that matches who you intend to be. These reps build reliability. When stakes rise, the pattern is already there.

1.3 The Quiet Tyrants: Ego, Impulse, and Status

Some forces don't announce themselves as enemies. They feel like helpers. Ego says, protect your image. Impulse says, relieve the discomfort now. Status says, don't fall behind. Left unchecked, these quiet tyrants run the city from the inside.

Ego flares at disrespect, real or imagined. It wants to correct, to dominate, to be seen as right. Impulse flares at uncertainty. It wants certainty now, even if borrowed or destructive. Status flares at comparison. It wants proof that you matter, preferably visible and immediate. None of these are evil; they evolved to protect. But protection without judgment becomes control.

Identify your default triggers. Be precise. Disrespect might show up when someone interrupts you. Uncertainty might spike when plans change. Comparison might activate when you see others advancing. Rejection might surface as silence or criticism. Name the trigger and the tyrant it feeds. This naming weakens their authority.

The most reliable antidote is a small pause. Not a dramatic retreat. A breath. A count to five. A sip of water. This is "delay before display." You delay the outward expression long enough to choose. Many regrets are not about what you felt; they are about what you showed too soon. A small pause prevents a large repair.

History is full of leaders undone not by lack of intelligence, but by impulse displayed at the wrong moment. A cutting remark. A hasty order. A public reaction that should have remained private.

The cost was rarely immediate; it compounded. The pause is not hesitation; it is governance.

Status deserves special attention because it hides behind ambition. Wanting to do well is healthy. Letting comparison dictate behavior is corrosive. Status says your worth is measured by rank, applause, or visibility. Integrity says your worth is measured by consistency with your values, especially when nobody is watching.

Redefine status as integrity. Ask who you are when there is no reward, no audience, no immediate payoff. Do you keep your word? Do you tell the truth kindly? Do you act with restraint when you could exploit? This definition stabilizes you. External markers can rise and fall without taking you with them.

Practice this redefinition in private moments. Return the cart. Close the loop on a promise that would be easy to forget. Speak up for someone who can't repay you. These actions train a status system that doesn't depend on comparison. You stop chasing signals and start building character.

Impulse will still knock. Ego will still flare. Status will still whisper. The work is not eradication; it is management. You acknowledge the signal, you pause, and you choose the response aligned with your values. Over time, the tyrants lose volume. The city runs quieter.

By the end of this chapter, you should feel something subtle but important: a shift from being pushed to being positioned. You haven't gained control over the weather. You've gained command of the citadel. In the next chapter, you'll learn how to fortify this command with daily practices that make clarity the default rather than the exception.

Chapter 2 — Clear Seeing: How to Think Without Fooling Yourself

"It is not things themselves that disturb us, but our judgments about them." — Epictetus

2.1 The Mind's Optical Illusions

Clear seeing is not a talent you're born with. It's a discipline you practice. The mind evolved to keep you alive, not to keep you accurate. Under pressure, it trades precision for speed. It fills gaps, predicts danger, and simplifies complexity. This kept our ancestors safe. Today, it often keeps us stressed, reactive, and wrong. The aim of this chapter is not to make you doubt every thought. It's to teach you how to recognize when the mind is distorting the picture—and how to correct course before you act on a mirage.

Think of the mind as a pair of glasses that can quietly warp your vision. When you forget you're wearing them, you assume what you see is reality itself. Clear seeing begins when you remember the glasses are there. You don't smash them. You clean them.

One common distortion is catastrophizing. This is the mind's habit of leaping from a small uncertainty to a large disaster. A delayed reply becomes a ruined relationship. A mistake becomes a career-ending flaw. A symptom becomes a dire diagnosis. The mind rushes to the worst-case scenario because it believes preparedness equals safety. The trouble is that living in worst-case mode taxes the nervous system and narrows choice. You end up responding to an imagined emergency instead of the actual situation.

Another illusion is mind-reading. You infer what others think or feel without sufficient evidence. A neutral tone becomes hostility. A short message becomes dismissal. Silence becomes rejection. The mind fills the gap with a story that matches your fear. You then react to that story as if it were confirmed truth. Relationships suffer not because of facts, but because of unchecked inferences.

Black-and-white thinking is subtler and just as costly. It reduces a spectrum into extremes. Success or failure. Loyal or disloyal. Right or wrong. When nuance disappears, so do options. You either double down or give up. This illusion feels decisive, but it's brittle. Reality tends to live in gradients. Learning to see shades restores flexibility.

Spotting these traps is not about labeling yourself as irrational. It's about recognizing patterns. When emotion spikes, ask which illusion is likely active. Is the mind forecasting disaster? Is it assuming knowledge it doesn't have? Is it collapsing complexity into an absolute? Naming the pattern interrupts it. You step out of the movie and back into the room.

A practical tool helps here: the three explanations rule. When something unsettling happens, the mind rushes to one explanation, usually the most threatening. Pause and generate three plausible stories before believing the first. Not three positive fantasies—three reasonable alternatives.

If someone cancels plans, the first story might be, "They don't value me." Generate two more: "Something urgent came up," or "They're overwhelmed and need rest." You don't need to decide which is true yet. The point is to loosen certainty. Certainty about a negative story is what fuels distress. Multiple explanations restore humility and calm.

This rule is powerful because it respects uncertainty instead of trying to eliminate it. You are not pretending everything is fine. You are refusing to convict reality on a single piece of circumstantial evidence. Historically, wise decision-makers did this instinctively. They delayed judgment until more information arrived, knowing that early certainty is often a disguise for fear.

Another foundational practice is separating facts from feelings. Feelings are real experiences, but they are not evidence about the world. When feelings are treated as facts, thinking warps. To counter this, use a simple two-column method. On one side, write what you observed. On the other, write how you interpreted it.

Observed might read: "The meeting started ten minutes late. Two people interrupted me." Interpreted might read: "They don't respect me. My input doesn't matter." Seeing these side by side is clarifying. The observation is concrete. The interpretation is a story layered on top. This doesn't mean the story is false. It means it's unproven.

Do this on paper or in your head. The physical act of separation matters. It slows the mind and restores proportion. Often, you'll notice how quickly interpretation escalates beyond observation. The gap between the two is where choice lives.

Eastern insight adds an important layer here: the mind clings to interpretations because it wants a stable self-image. If the story is "I'm undervalued," then the self becomes a victim or a fighter. These identities feel solid, even when painful. Letting go of the story can feel like losing ground. Clear seeing requires courage because it loosens identities that were built to protect you.

Stoic practice counters this by reminding you that judgment is optional. Events present data. Judgment assigns meaning. You can choose to delay that assignment. Delay is not denial. It's accuracy. When you delay judgment, you create room for better information and better responses.

Use these tools in real time, not just reflection. When your chest tightens after reading a message, pause. Name the illusion likely at work. Generate three explanations. Separate observation from interpretation. Then decide what action, if any, is needed. Often, the right action is to wait. Waiting is an action when it prevents error.

Clear seeing also requires recognizing confirmation bias—the mind's tendency to notice evidence that supports its current story and ignore what doesn't. If you believe you're failing, you'll collect every misstep and discount progress. If you believe someone is against you, you'll scan for slights and miss support. The remedy is intentional counter-evidence. Ask, "What would I notice if the opposite were true?" This question widens perception without forcing optimism.

The goal is not to become perfectly objective. That's impossible. The goal is to become less fooled by your first impression. You move from reflex to review. From assumption to inquiry. This shift alone reduces conflict, regret, and wasted energy.

Practice this when stakes are low. When choosing a restaurant. When interpreting a tone. When traffic slows. Each rep trains the same skill you'll need when stakes are high. Over time, you'll notice a calmer baseline. Fewer emotional spikes. Quicker recovery. Not because life is easier, but because you see it more accurately.

Clear seeing is an act of respect—for reality and for yourself. Reality doesn't need your distortion to function. You don't need distortion to act. When you clean the lens, decisions improve naturally.

In the next section, you'll learn how to test your judgments against reality through small experiments, turning clear seeing into a habit that strengthens with use rather than fading under pressure.

2.2 Eastern Clarity: The Observer and the Passing Thought

Clear seeing deepens when you realize a simple truth: you are aware of your thoughts, but you are not your thoughts. This is not a metaphysical claim. It is a practical one. The moment you can observe a thought, you are already one step removed from it. Eastern traditions built entire systems around this insight, not to escape life, but to live it with less distortion.

Begin with a practice called noting. It is deliberately plain. When a thought arises, you label it with a single word and move on. "Worry." "Planning." "Anger." "Remembering." The label is not analysis. It's a tag. By tagging the thought, you reduce fusion—the sense that the thought is you or that it must be acted on immediately. The mind relaxes when it's seen.

Try this during a stressful moment. The mind says, "This is going to go badly." Instead of arguing, note "catastrophizing" or simply "worry." Then return attention to something neutral and present. The breath. The sensation of your hands. The task in front of you. The thought may return. Label it again. Each label is a rep. Over time, the thought loses urgency. Not because you defeated it, but because you stopped feeding it with identity.

Impermanence is the second insight to practice—not as philosophy, but as observation. Emotions feel solid when you're inside them. Anger feels like truth. Anxiety feels like foresight. Sadness feels like permanence. Watch closely and you'll see they move. They rise, peak, and pass. Sometimes quickly. Sometimes slowly. Always eventually.

Treat emotions as weather patterns, not identities. Rain is real. It changes what you do. It does not become who you are. When you say "I am anxious," you turn a passing state into a fixed self. When you say "Anxiety is here," you create room. This small linguistic shift restores agency. You can carry an umbrella without declaring yourself a storm.

This perspective prevents secondary suffering. Primary suffering is the emotion itself. Secondary suffering is the story you add: "I shouldn't feel this," or "This means something is wrong with me." Let the weather pass without commentary. Prepare. Adjust. Continue.

Breath is the most reliable reset switch you have. Not because breathing solves problems, but because it returns you to choice. One minute of attentive breathing changes the body's signal from threat to availability. Count ten slow breaths. Feel the exhale lengthen. The mind follows the body. When the body softens, interpretation follows.

Use breath strategically. Before sending a message. After receiving unexpected news. When irritation spikes. One minute is enough to prevent a reflex you'll have to clean up later. This is not retreat; it's leadership of your own system.

The observer stance does not make you passive. It makes you precise. You see the thought, you see the feeling, and you decide the response. This is freedom in practice. Not freedom from experience, but freedom within it.

2.3 Historical Skepticism: Evidence, Incentives, and Power

Clear seeing also requires skepticism—not cynicism, but disciplined doubt. History teaches that many confident claims were wrong, not because people were stupid, but because incentives skewed truth. When stakes are high, narratives serve interests. To think clearly, you must ask better questions.

Start with a simple one: who benefits if I believe this? Not in a paranoid way. In a practical one. If a story increases fear, does it sell protection? If it inflames outrage, does it consolidate power? If it promises effortless success, does it recruit attention or money? This question does not prove falsehood. It flags motivation. Motivation matters.

Next, apply the source triangle. Evaluate three things before granting belief. Competence: does the source understand the subject? Incentives: do they gain from persuading you? Proximity to facts: are they close to the evidence or repeating hearsay? A source can be sincere and still unreliable. Another can be biased and still occasionally right. The triangle helps you weigh, not worship.

History rewards those who asked these questions early. Skeptics noticed when certainty outpaced evidence. They delayed commitment until claims survived scrutiny. This wasn't indecision; it was prudence. Strong opinions require strong evidence. Weak evidence earns provisional belief at best.

Intellectual humility is not self-doubt. It's calibration. You can act decisively while holding beliefs lightly. You say, "Based on what I know now, this seems likely," and you stay open to update. This stance prevents embarrassment and enables learning.

Practice humility in everyday judgments. When you feel sure about someone's intent, check the triangle. When a claim fits your preferences perfectly, raise the bar for evidence. When everyone around you agrees, look for missing data. Consensus can be comforting and wrong.

Clear seeing, then, is layered. You clean internal lenses with observation and breath. You clean external lenses with skepticism and evidence. Together, they reduce error.

By the end of this chapter, you should feel less compelled to rush to judgment. Not because you hesitate, but because you see more. In the next chapter, you'll learn how to turn clear seeing into wise action—how to decide and move forward without waiting for perfect certainty.

Chapter 3 — Desire, Attachment, and Enough

"He is richest who is content with the least." — Socrates

3.1 Stoic Desire: Want Less, Own More of Yourself

Desire is not the enemy. Unexamined desire is. Most of what exhausts you is not effort, but craving—wanting things to be different before you allow yourself to be at ease. The Stoics understood this clearly. They didn't preach denial or austerity for its own sake. They taught something far more practical: when desire runs unchecked, it owns you; when desire is trained, you regain possession of your time, attention, and peace.

Start by noticing how often your mood depends on getting something. A response, a result, a purchase, recognition, progress. The mind says, "Once this happens, then I'll settle." This creates a permanent forward lean. Life becomes a series of thresholds you keep crossing without ever arriving. Contentment is always postponed.

Stoic desire flips this logic. Instead of asking, "How can I get more?" it asks, "How little do I need to be steady?" This is not resignation. It is leverage. The fewer conditions you require to be okay, the more resilient you become. You stop being negotiable.

The first step is identifying borrowed desires. These are wants you did not consciously choose. They were handed to you by culture, family, peers, or algorithms. Status scripts tell you what success should look like, what timeline you should follow, what signals matter. You absorb these scripts early and often without consent.

Borrowed desire sounds like urgency without clarity. You want something badly, but if asked why, your answer is vague or circular. "Because that's what people do." "Because I don't want to fall behind." "Because it proves something." The desire is loud, but its value is thin.

Pause and examine one strong want in your life right now. Ask where it came from. Not who benefits if you have it, but who benefits if you want it. Often the answer is not you. Advertising thrives on borrowed desire. Comparison feeds on it. Entire industries depend on convincing you that your current state is insufficient.

This doesn't mean the object of desire is wrong. It means the motivation deserves inspection. A goal driven by borrowed desire costs more energy than it returns. Even if you achieve it, the satisfaction is brief, followed by the next script.

Stoic practice recommends voluntary simplicity as a counterweight. This does not mean selling everything or living harshly. It means periodically choosing less on purpose. You skip something you could easily afford. You delay a purchase. You choose a simpler option without self-punishment. These are small acts, but they retrain the nervous system.

Voluntary simplicity teaches your body that you will be okay without immediate gratification. Craving weakens when it is not constantly obeyed. You discover that the discomfort of not having fades faster than expected. Freedom grows in the space where compulsion used to live.

Try a simple experiment. For one week, choose one "less." Less sugar. Less scrolling. Less buying. Less explaining yourself. Notice what happens. At first, the mind protests. It invents reasons. Then it quiets. Energy returns. Attention sharpens. You haven't lost pleasure; you've removed noise.

Eastern insight complements this by distinguishing desire from attachment. Desire says, "I would enjoy this." Attachment says, "I need this to be okay." The suffering comes from the second. You can want without clinging. You can pursue without being owned by outcome.

Stoic desire is not about suppressing enjoyment. It's about removing desperation. When you are not desperate, you choose better. You negotiate from strength. You walk away when terms degrade your values. You enjoy what arrives without demanding it stay.

This leads to the deepest shift: replacing wanting with valuing. Wanting is future-oriented and restless. Valuing is present-oriented and grounding. When you value something, you care for it. You protect it. You notice it. You don't constantly demand it be different.

Shift from acquisition to appreciation. Instead of asking what else you need, ask what you already have that deserves fuller attention. This is not forced gratitude. It's precision. Appreciation is a skill of noticing what is already supporting you—your body's capacity, a stable relationship, a skill you've earned, a quiet morning.

Appreciation does not make you complacent. It stabilizes you so growth is chosen rather than frantic. When you appreciate your current position, you make clearer decisions about what to change and what to keep. You stop confusing motion with progress.

Historically, many who accumulated the most power or wealth also learned restraint early. They understood that appetite without limits invites capture. Capture by excess, by fear of loss, by the need to defend what was gained. Enough is not a number. It's a relationship with desire.

Ask yourself a grounding question: if this desire were fulfilled, what would it give me emotionally? Peace? Respect? Freedom? Then ask whether there is a simpler way to cultivate that state without waiting. Often there is. Peace through order. Respect through competence. Freedom through fewer obligations.

Owning more of yourself means reclaiming attention from endless wanting. It means you decide what matters rather than reacting to what is marketed or modeled. It means you enjoy success without making it your identity and endure loss without making it your verdict.

This is a quiet power. Others may not notice immediately. But you will. Decisions feel lighter. Comparisons lose heat. You stop chasing proof and start building substance.

In the next section, you'll learn how attachment forms—not just to things, but to identities and outcomes—and how loosening that grip does not make life smaller, but far more spacious.

3.2 Eastern Attachment: The Grip That Creates Suffering

Desire turns into suffering when it tightens into attachment. Eastern traditions describe attachment as a grip—a subtle contraction around outcomes that turns preference into requirement. You don't just want something; you need it to confirm who you are. When the need is threatened, the body reacts as if the self were under attack. Anxiety rises. Anger sharpens. Flexibility disappears.

Clinging is easiest to spot not in what you chase, but in how you react when the chase is interrupted. Notice the spike when a plan changes, when recognition doesn't arrive, when effort isn't rewarded on your timeline. That spike is not proof that the goal matters; it's evidence that validation is riding on the outcome.

Ask yourself a clarifying question: what would this outcome say about me if it worked? Successful? Lovable? Safe? Respected? Now ask the harder follow-up: what would it say if it didn't? Often the answer is harsh and absolute. Failure becomes a verdict. Delay becomes a dismissal. This is attachment at work—turning events into identity.

Eastern practice does not tell you to stop caring. It teaches you to care with an open hand. Open-hand goals are commitments to effort without a demand for control. You show up fully. You prepare. You practice. You persist. And you release the insistence that reality must comply on your schedule or in your preferred form.

An open-hand goal sounds like this: "I will train consistently and submit my work, and I release the outcome." Or, "I will speak honestly and kindly, and I release how it is received." This stance preserves dignity. You remain intact regardless of result. Effort becomes yours; outcomes remain weather.

This does not reduce ambition. It purifies it. You stop bargaining with fate and start investing in craft. You discover that much of the pressure you felt was self-imposed—a tax for demanding certainty where none exists.

Training equanimity is the daily practice that makes open-hand goals possible. Equanimity is not indifference. It is balance. You meet pleasure and pain without losing your center. When something good happens, you enjoy it without clinging. When something painful happens, you respond without collapse.

A simple way to train equanimity is to notice your inner commentary after wins and losses. After a win, does the mind rush to protect it, to repeat it, to announce it? After a loss, does it rush to explain, to blame, to withdraw? Gently interrupt both. Let pleasure be pleasant without becoming a standard you must maintain. Let pain be painful without becoming a story about your worth.

Breath and body awareness support this training. When emotion surges, return to sensation. Feel the contact points. Lengthen the exhale. The body steadies first; the mind follows. You are not suppressing feeling. You are keeping your footing while it passes.

Equanimity grows with repetition. Small disappointments are training grounds. Missed opportunities. Awkward moments. Minor setbacks. Meet them with the same open hand you intend to use when stakes rise. Over time, the grip loosens. You still care. You are simply harder to shake.

3.3 Historical Wealth: Luxury, Decay, and Discipline

History offers a clear pattern that repeats across eras. Comfort rises. Restraint falls. Character thins. Societies and individuals alike confuse ease with stability and abundance with security. The result is fragility. When conditions change—as they always do—those who abandoned discipline struggle to adapt.

Luxury is not the villain. Unexamined luxury is. Comfort dulls the edge that once kept skills sharp and values active. When everything is easy, the muscles that manage difficulty atrophy. When difficulty returns, it feels unbearable, not because it is unprecedented, but because preparation was abandoned.

Wise cultures and individuals countered this with discipline during good times. They kept practices that reminded them of limits. They maintained routines that did not depend on external pressure. They trained for adversity while enjoying prosperity. This is not pessimism; it is realism.

Build anti-fragile habits—habits that strengthen under both comfort and strain. Physical movement that continues regardless of mood. Clear thinking practices that don't vanish when life is smooth. Financial restraint that persists even when income rises. Honest feedback loops that survive success.

Anti-fragile habits are boring when things are easy. That's the point. They keep you grounded when novelty fades. They also become lifelines when circumstances tighten. You don't scramble to invent character under pressure; you reveal what you've practiced.

Creating your personal definition of "enough" is the anchor that stops the endless chase. Enough is not asceticism. It's clarity. Decide what resources, recognition, and comfort actually support your values. Everything beyond that is optional, not compulsory.

Write your definition in plain language. Enough money to cover needs and create margin. Enough status to do meaningful work without contorting yourself. Enough comfort to rest well without dulling ambition. This definition is allowed to evolve, but it must be conscious.

Without a definition of enough, desire expands to fill any container. The finish line moves. Satisfaction recedes. With a definition, you can enjoy gains without becoming addicted to them. You can say no without fear. You can choose projects for meaning, not just momentum.

Historically, those who endured were not those with the most, but those with standards that did not inflate with success. They kept rituals of restraint. They remembered what was sufficient. They understood that freedom is not having everything, but needing little to stand steady.

As you integrate this chapter, notice where desire has been driving and where it can serve instead. Notice where attachment tightens and where it can loosen. Notice where enough has been undefined and decide it deliberately.

In the next chapter, you will learn how to translate this steadiness into action—how to decide and move forward with clarity when options multiply and certainty remains elusive.

Chapter 4 — Emotion as Information: Anger, Fear, and Grief With Skill

"Between stimulus and response there is a space." — often attributed to Viktor Frankl

4.1 Fear: A Prediction, Not a Prophecy

Fear feels like certainty. It arrives with urgency, tightens the body, and presents a vivid picture of what might go wrong. The problem is not that fear appears. The problem is that it pretends to be a prophet. When fear speaks, it doesn't say, "Here is one possible outcome." It says, "This is what will happen." Clear emotional skill begins when you learn to hear fear as information, not instruction.

Fear is a prediction engine. Its job is to scan for threat and prepare you to respond. That job is ancient and useful. But like any system designed for survival, it errs on the side of false positives. It would rather alarm you ten times unnecessarily than miss one real danger. Understanding this changes your relationship with fear. You stop arguing with it and start interrogating it.

The first tool is the probability drill. When fear paints a scenario, ask two separate questions: what is possible, and what is likely? Fear collapses these into one. It treats the worst case as the default. Your task is to separate them calmly.

Possibility is broad. Many things are possible. You could fail. You could be rejected. You could lose money. You could get hurt. Acknowledging possibility is honest. Likelihood is narrower. It requires data. How often has this actually happened before? What are the base rates? What evidence do you have right now, not in imagination?

Run this drill on paper or in your head. Fear says, "This will go badly." You respond, "What specifically am I afraid of?" Name it precisely. Then ask, "How likely is this outcome, realistically?" Not zero or one hundred. Use a range. Ten percent. Thirty percent. This alone reduces intensity. The nervous system relaxes when uncertainty is quantified instead of dramatized.

Next, ask what the most likely outcome is. Often it's mundane. Not great. Not catastrophic. Just uncomfortable. Fear thrives on vagueness. Specificity weakens it.

The second skill is shrinking fear through action. Fear feeds on rumination. The more you think without moving, the more elaborate the prediction becomes. Action interrupts this loop. Not heroic action. Small, brave steps.

Choose the smallest action that moves you toward the feared domain. Send the email. Make the call. Open the document. Ask the question. One step is enough. The body learns faster than the mind. When you act and survive, fear updates its model. Rumination stops because the system receives new data.

This is why procrastination intensifies fear. Avoidance starves the brain of corrective experience. The mind fills the gap with imagined threats. Movement, even minimal, restores proportion.

Historical accounts of courage consistently show this pattern. Soldiers, explorers, reformers did not wait for fear to disappear. They moved while afraid, often in small increments, and fear adjusted. Courage is not the absence of fear. It is fear informed by action.

The third practice is premeditation, a Stoic technique often misunderstood. Premeditation does not mean dwelling on disaster. It means calmly rehearsing difficulty so that it doesn't shock you when it appears. Shock amplifies fear. Familiarity reduces it.

Set aside a short, contained time. Five minutes. Imagine a difficulty you might reasonably face. Not the most extreme fantasy, but a plausible challenge. Picture it clearly. Then ask, "If this happened, what would I do?" Walk through the steps. Who would you contact? What resources would you use? What would remain intact?

This rehearsal does two things. It separates fear from helplessness, and it builds confidence without bravado. You discover that even in adverse scenarios, there are options. The future becomes less opaque. When something similar occurs, the body recognizes the terrain. Fear still appears, but it's quieter.

Eastern traditions pair this with acceptance. You do not rehearse to control outcomes. You rehearse to meet them. The aim is readiness, not dominance. You accept that some discomfort is part of a full life. Resistance decreases. Energy returns.

Use premeditation sparingly. Once or twice a week. Keep it brief. End by returning attention to the present. You are not training anxiety; you are training preparedness.

A final refinement matters: fear often signals value. You are afraid because something matters—reputation, safety, belonging, purpose. Respect the signal without surrendering to the story. Ask what value is being threatened and how to protect it wisely. Sometimes the answer is caution. Sometimes it's courage. Fear does not decide. You do.

As you practice these skills, fear changes texture. It becomes a nudge rather than a shove. An advisor rather than a tyrant. You feel it sooner and respond with more skill.

In the next section, you will learn to work with anger—how to hear what it protects, how to express it without damage, and how to turn its energy into constructive force.

4.2 Anger: The Desire to Punish Reality

Anger feels justified. It arrives with heat, speed, and a clear narrative: something is wrong, and someone should pay. At its core, anger is the desire to punish reality for not matching your expectations. This does not make anger bad. It makes it informative. When understood, anger points to a boundary, a value, or an expectation that was violated. When misunderstood, it burns bridges and clouds judgment.

Begin by identifying the expectation underneath the anger. Not the accusation on the surface, but the rule you assumed was in place. "People should be fair." "I should be respected." "This should have gone as planned." Anger spikes when reality breaks a rule you didn't know you were enforcing. Naming the rule brings the emotion into focus.

This step alone cools the system. Instead of, "They're incompetent," you arrive at, "I expected reliability." Instead of, "This is unacceptable," you see, "I expected transparency." Expectations are negotiable; moral verdicts are not. Once named, you can decide whether the expectation was reasonable, whether it was communicated, and how to respond now.

Stoic practice emphasizes this pause. The initial surge is involuntary. The second surge—the one fueled by judgment—is optional. You cannot stop anger from arising, but you can prevent it from driving.

A powerful method here is steel-man then speak. Before you respond, state the other side's best argument as clearly and fairly as you can. Not a straw version. The strongest version. This does two things. It proves to yourself that you understand the full picture, and it slows the impulse to punish.

If you can articulate the other side's rationale, even when you disagree, your response becomes precise instead of explosive. You move from accusation to dialogue. This does not mean you concede. It means you engage with reality rather than a caricature.

When you do speak, choose firmness without heat. Heat feels powerful, but it confuses the message. Boundaries land more clearly when they are calm. "This doesn't work for me." "I need reliability here." "I'm not willing to continue under these conditions." These statements are harder to dismiss because they are not performances; they are positions.

Historically, effective leaders understood this. Public fury rallied crowds briefly; steady firmness changed systems. Anger spent in explosions burns fuel without moving the structure. Anger channeled into boundaries reshapes behavior over time.

Practice this in small interactions. When interrupted, say, "I'd like to finish my thought." When plans change, say, "I need earlier notice." Each calm boundary trains the system. Anger still signals, but it no longer hijacks.

Over time, you'll notice something surprising. The less you explode, the less anger accumulates. Much of chronic anger comes from unexpressed boundaries. Clear expression prevents buildup. You don't need to punish reality when you can negotiate with it.

4.3 Grief and Impermanence: Loving Without Possessing

Grief is the price of love. It is not a malfunction to be fixed or a weakness to overcome. It is evidence that something mattered deeply. Cultures that tried to bypass grief often ended up brittle. Cultures that gave grief form found resilience.

Allow grief without rushing it. The impulse to "move on" is often discomfort with feeling, not readiness. Grief moves in waves. Some days are functional. Some are heavy. This variability is normal. When you allow grief its rhythm, it integrates rather than lingers.

Eastern insight teaches impermanence not as detachment, but as honesty. Everything you love will change or end. Knowing this does not make love smaller; it makes it more tender. You love without possessing. You appreciate without demanding permanence.

Ritual gives grief a container. Historically, rituals marked loss because emotion needs form to move. Without form, grief spills into unrelated areas—irritability, numbness, exhaustion. Create simple rituals. Light a candle on certain days. Write a letter you don't send. Walk a familiar route and remember. These acts tell the body, "This has a place."

Ritual does not trap you in the past. It prevents grief from haunting the present. When honored, grief softens.

The final transformation is converting pain into virtue. Ask a difficult, dignifying question: what kind of person does this loss call you to be? More patient. More present. More generous. More honest. Loss can shrink you or refine you. The difference is choice.

This does not mean you justify the loss. It means you refuse to waste it. You let love continue as character. This is how grief becomes meaning without becoming a slogan.

As you complete this chapter, notice how emotions shift when treated as information rather than commands. Fear advises. Anger signals boundaries. Grief testifies to love. None of them need to rule. In the next chapter, you'll learn how to translate this emotional intelligence into wise decisions under pressure.

Chapter 5 — Time and Mortality: The Sharpening Stone

"You could leave life right now. Let that determine what you do."
— Marcus Aurelius

5.1 Memento Mori as a Life-Design Tool

Most people treat mortality as a threat to be avoided, a thought to push away so life can continue undisturbed. The Stoics treated it differently. They used it as a sharpening stone. Not to darken the mind, but to focus it. When you remember that time is finite, the trivial loses its grip and the essential comes forward on its own. You don't need motivation; you gain clarity.

Memento mori—remember you will die—is often misunderstood as morbid. Practiced correctly, it is grounding. It brings decisions into proportion. When everything feels urgent, nothing is. When time is visible, priorities organize themselves.

Begin with last day clarity. Imagine, calmly and without drama, that today were your last ordinary day. Not your last hour in a hospital bed, but your last day with agency. You can move, speak, choose. What becomes obvious immediately? Which worries dissolve? Which conversations feel necessary? Which tasks feel absurd? This is not a fantasy exercise; it's a diagnostic.

Notice how quickly certain concerns lose authority. The email thread. The argument you keep rehearsing. The comparison that usually stings. Mortality exposes their smallness without you having to reason it away. At the same time, other things gain weight. Showing up fully for someone. Finishing something meaningful. Speaking honestly. Being present.

This clarity is always available. You don't need a crisis to access it. You need a reminder. Practice this once a week. Five minutes is enough. Let the answers come without forcing them. Write down what becomes obvious. Over time, patterns appear. Those patterns are your values trying to speak.

The next step is subtraction. When time is limited, you don't add more; you cut what doesn't matter. Most exhaustion comes not from doing hard things, but from doing many unaligned things. Cut trivia, not joy.

Trivia are obligations that consume energy without expressing your values. Meetings that exist out of habit. Commitments you accepted to avoid discomfort. Roles that once fit but no longer do. These drain you because they dilute attention.

Joy is different. Joy may be demanding. It may require effort. It may even be tiring in a clean way. But it replenishes meaning. Distinguish between clean tired and dirty tired. Clean tired follows work that mattered. Dirty tired follows compliance.

Use mortality as a filter. If time were short, would you keep this obligation? If not, why is it here now? You don't need to eliminate everything at once. Start with one subtraction. Say no where you used to say yes by default. Create space. Space is not emptiness; it's capacity.

Historically, those who lived with a sense of finitude did not rush less; they rushed more selectively. They chose depth over breadth. They did fewer things and did them with care. This is not laziness. It's respect for time.

The final tool in this section is the deathbed sentence. One line. No accolades. No titles. Just how you want to be remembered by those who knew you well. "She was generous with her attention." "He stood for what mattered, even when it cost him." "They made people feel seen." This sentence is not a performance for others; it's a compass for you.

Write it plainly. Then test your current schedule against it. Does your week support this sentence? Not perfectly. Not always. But directionally. If not, adjust. This is how mortality becomes design, not dread.

Memento mori does not make life bleak. It makes it sharp. It reminds you that postponement is a choice, and so is presence. When you remember you could leave at any time, you stop living as if you have unlimited drafts.

In the next section, you'll learn how to translate this clarity into daily time stewardship—how to spend your hours in ways that honor both urgency and rest without burning out.

5.2 Eastern Time: Presence as Depth

Western culture tends to treat time as a resource to be managed, optimized, and squeezed. Eastern traditions approach time differently. They treat it as an experience to be entered fully. The shift from management to presence changes everything. When you are present, time deepens. When you are scattered, time thins. The same hour can feel empty or rich depending on how you inhabit it.

The first practice is one-tasking. This sounds obvious and feels radical because it runs against habit. One-tasking means giving undivided attention to the single thing you are doing right now. Not half-attention while planning the next thing. Not performance for an imagined audience. Just this.

Multitasking creates the illusion of efficiency while quietly eroding depth. Attention fractures. Errors increase. Satisfaction drops. One-tasking restores integrity. When you give something full attention, you experience it more clearly and complete it more cleanly. The mind relaxes when it's not constantly switching.

Start small. Choose one daily activity to do with full presence. Washing dishes. Writing an email. Walking to the store. Put the phone away. Feel the sensations. Notice the movements. You're not adding time; you're reclaiming it. Depth accumulates without effort.

This leads to the practice of the ordinary sacred. Sacred does not mean solemn or religious. It means worthy of attention. Eastern traditions noticed that meaning does not require special circumstances. It requires awareness. When you bring awareness to ordinary acts, they stop being placeholders between "important" moments and become the fabric of life.

Drinking tea. Brushing teeth. Opening a door. These acts anchor you. When treated as sacred, they interrupt autopilot. Autopilot is where time disappears. Awareness is where it returns.

Choose one ordinary act and elevate it. Not with ceremony, but with care. Do it the same way each time. Let it mark a transition—into work, into rest, into sleep. Over time, these anchors structure your day gently. You don't rush through life; you arrive at it repeatedly.

Micro-sabbaths are the final practice here. A sabbath is a pause that restores meaning. You don't need a day. You need moments. Thirty seconds between tasks. Two minutes of stillness before a meeting. A short walk after lunch without stimulation. These pauses reset the nervous system and remind you that life is not only output.

Micro-sabbaths prevent burnout because they break the trance of urgency. Urgency feels productive but exhausts meaning. Pauses reintroduce choice. You remember why you're doing what you're doing.

Build these pauses deliberately. Schedule them if needed. Treat them as non-negotiable, like hydration for the mind. Over time, they accumulate into a calmer baseline. You move through days with less friction and more presence.

5.3 Historical Time: How Great Lives Are Built

History reveals a quiet truth that contradicts modern myth: great lives are rarely built through dramatic bursts. They are built through long arcs of boring consistency. What looks like genius or destiny from the outside is usually discipline sustained over time.

Study any enduring achievement and you'll find repetition. The same skills practiced daily. The same principles applied patiently. The same standards upheld when nobody is watching. This is not glamorous. It is effective.

The compounding effect explains why. Small decisions, repeated, become character. Character shapes choices. Choices shape outcomes. Over years, the curve bends. What felt insignificant becomes decisive.

Track this in your own life. Notice the small decisions you repeat. How you speak when tired. How you spend the first hour of the day. How you respond to discomfort. These are not trivial. They are votes for the kind of person you are becoming.

Adopt a cathedral mindset. Medieval cathedrals were built over generations. The builders knew they would not see the finished work. They built anyway. With care. With pride. With faith in continuity. This mindset frees you from mood-driven effort.

Ask what you are building that outlasts your current emotions. A body of work. A relationship culture. A reputation for integrity. Systems that support others. These require patience. Some days you won't feel like building. You build anyway, lightly but consistently.

This mindset reduces anxiety about speed. You stop asking, "How fast can I get there?" and start asking, "Is this worthy of years?" The answer guides what you accept and what you decline.

Historical figures who endured did not chase constant novelty. They deepened commitments. They returned to the same craft. They refined rather than replaced. This is how mastery emerges.

As you integrate this chapter, notice how your relationship with time shifts. From enemy to teacher. From pressure to guide. Mortality sharpens choices. Presence deepens experience. Consistency builds legacy.

In the next chapter, you'll learn how to align your actions with your values under real-world constraints—how to act with integrity when trade-offs are unavoidable and time is limited.

Chapter 6 — Character: Virtue as the Only Real Security

"Waste no more time arguing what a good person should be. Be one." — Marcus Aurelius

6.1 Stoic Virtues: Wisdom, Courage, Justice, Temperance

When conditions are uncertain—and they always are—character is the only security that doesn't depreciate. Skills can become obsolete. Status can evaporate. Plans can collapse. Character remains portable. It goes with you into any room, any season, any loss. The Stoics did not treat virtue as moral decoration. They treated it as infrastructure. When everything else shakes, virtue holds.

The word "virtue" can sound abstract or old-fashioned, as if it belongs in a lecture rather than a life. Strip away the abstraction and you're left with something practical: virtue is how you behave when no rulebook covers the situation. It's what guides you when incentives are mixed, information is incomplete, and emotions are loud. Virtue is not about being good in theory; it's about being reliable in practice.

The Stoic framework centers on four virtues—wisdom, courage, justice, and temperance. They are not traits you either have or don't. They are skills you practice. Each one answers a different kind of pressure you'll face today.

Wisdom is not intelligence. It's judgment. Wisdom is the ability to see what matters, what doesn't, and what to do next. In daily life, wisdom looks like asking better questions before acting. It looks like pausing long enough to distinguish signal from noise. When an email provokes you, wisdom asks what outcome you actually want. When a choice is complex, wisdom narrows it to first principles.

Convert wisdom into behavior by practicing clarity. Before acting, state the goal in one sentence. If you can't, you're not ready to act. Clarify constraints. Name the trade-off you're accepting. Wisdom is not certainty; it's coherence. You know why you're choosing what you're choosing, and you're willing to own the cost.

Courage is not fearlessness. It's movement with fear present. Courage shows up when comfort pulls one way and values pull another. In daily life, courage looks like speaking when silence would be easier, or listening when defensiveness would be easier. It looks like starting before you feel ready and stopping when continuing would compromise integrity.

Translate courage into behavior by identifying avoidance. What are you postponing that you already know you should address? A conversation. A decision. A boundary. Courage is rarely dramatic. It's often a single sentence delivered calmly. Practice courage in small doses so it's available when stakes rise.

Justice is not abstract fairness. It's how you treat people when power dynamics are uneven. Justice asks whether your actions respect the dignity of others, even when it costs you convenience. In daily life, justice looks like giving credit accurately, sharing information honestly, and refusing to benefit from another's blind spot.

Behaviorally, justice shows up in how you speak about people who aren't present. It shows up in whether you use rules to protect the vulnerable or to excuse yourself. It shows up in consistency—holding yourself to the same standard you expect from others. Justice is not softness. It's steadiness.

Temperance is the most misunderstood virtue. It's often mistaken for denial. In practice, temperance is proportion. It's knowing when enough is enough. In daily life, temperance looks like stopping before excess dulls judgment—whether the excess is food, work, stimulation, spending, or even self-improvement.

Convert temperance into behavior by setting gentle limits and honoring them. Decide in advance what "enough" looks like in one area and practice stopping there. Temperance preserves energy. It keeps desire from becoming compulsion. It protects future you from present impulse.

These virtues work together. Wisdom decides. Courage acts. Justice aligns actions with fairness. Temperance keeps the system balanced. When one is missing, the others distort. Courage without wisdom becomes recklessness. Wisdom without courage becomes paralysis. Justice without temperance becomes rigidity. Temperance without justice becomes self-absorption.

To make virtue usable under pressure, use virtue prompts. Before a decision, especially a charged one, ask a single targeted question. What would wisdom do here? What would courage say out loud? What would justice require if roles were reversed?

What would temperance limit right now? You don't need all four every time. Choose the one most relevant to the pressure you're feeling.

These prompts interrupt autopilot. They create a small space between impulse and action—the same space you've practiced throughout this book. Over time, the questions become reflexive. You don't deliberate longer; you deliberate better.

Virtue also needs feedback. Not praise or punishment, but reflection. Create a virtue scoreboard—not to grade yourself, but to notice patterns. At the end of the day, recall one moment where you expressed a virtue and one where you missed it. No self-criticism. No justification. Just data.

This reflection builds awareness without shame. Shame makes virtue theatrical. Awareness makes it consistent. You're not trying to be perfect. You're trying to be a little more aligned tomorrow than you were today.

Eastern traditions support this with the idea of practice over identity. You are not a courageous person; you practice courage. You are not a just person; you practice justice. This removes the pressure to defend an image. When you fail, you return to practice. Character strengthens through return, not perfection.

Historically, those remembered for character were not flawless. They were predictable in the right ways. People knew what they stood for. They trusted their responses under stress. This trust is earned slowly and lost quickly. Virtue protects it.

As you work with this chapter, notice where you've outsourced security—to approval, to control, to accumulation. Bring it back to character. Ask what kind of person you want to be when conditions are unfavorable. Then practice being that person in small, ordinary moments.

In the next section, you'll learn how to apply virtue when values collide—when there is no clean choice and trade-offs are real. That is where character stops being theory and becomes destiny.

6.2 Eastern Ethics: Compassion Without Weakness

Compassion is often misunderstood as softness, as if caring requires surrendering judgment or boundaries. Eastern ethics draw a sharper distinction. Compassion is the willingness to reduce suffering—yours and others'—without abandoning clarity. Weakness is what happens when compassion forgets limits. Strength is compassion guided by wisdom.

Begin with compassion with boundaries. Care does not require self-erasure. You can understand someone's pain without absorbing it. You can offer support without agreeing to mistreatment. Boundaries are not punishments; they are instructions for how to relate. When boundaries are clear, compassion can flow without resentment.

Notice where compassion turns into overextension. You say yes when you mean no. You explain excessively. You tolerate patterns that drain you and call it kindness. This is not compassion; it is fear of discomfort wearing a moral costume. True compassion includes yourself. It recognizes that depleted helpers help poorly.

Practice boundary language that is both kind and firm. "I can't do that, but I hope you find support." "I understand why this is hard, and I'm not available for this." These sentences honor reality. They reduce suffering by preventing confusion and false hope. Over time, they build trust because they are consistent.

Speech is a powerful site of non-harm. Words can escalate pain or ease it. Eastern ethics emphasize right speech—not perfect speech, but intentional speech. Before you speak, consider whether your words are true, necessary, and timely. You don't need to meet all three every time, but aiming for them reduces collateral damage.

Train non-harm in everyday conversations. Avoid exaggeration when upset. Avoid labels that freeze people into identities. Replace "always" and "never" with specifics. Speak about behavior rather than character. This doesn't weaken your position; it strengthens it. Precision lands. Broad condemnation provokes defense.

Tone matters as much as content. A calm tone communicates safety even when the message is firm. You are not responsible for others' reactions, but you are responsible for your delivery. Non-harm does not mean silence; it means choosing words that do not inflame unnecessarily.

Expand the circle of understanding without excusing harm. Eastern insight invites you to see people as conditioned by history, fear, incentives, and habits. This perspective does not deny responsibility. It contextualizes it. When you see conditioning, hatred loses heat. You respond to behavior rather than inventing monsters.

This shift protects your own mind. When you believe others are "evil by nature," you invite cynicism and despair. When you see conditioning, you retain agency. You can oppose actions firmly while keeping your humanity intact. This is how compassion and strength coexist.

Practice this lens in minor annoyances. The rude driver. The short reply. The missed deadline. Ask what pressures might be shaping behavior. You don't need to be right. You need to stay balanced. Balance preserves judgment.

Compassion without weakness is sustainable. It allows you to show up repeatedly without burning out. It keeps your character intact when others lose theirs. It is not passive. It is disciplined care.

6.3 Historical Honor: Reputation vs. Integrity

History draws a clear line between reputation and integrity. Reputation is what people think when you're not in the room. Integrity is who you are when nobody is watching. Reputation can be managed. Integrity must be practiced. The two overlap, but they are not the same.

Many failures—personal and political—began when reputation replaced integrity as the primary aim. Leaders protected image at the expense of truth. Individuals chased approval at the expense of values. Short-term praise masked long-term decay.

Separate public image from private truth deliberately. Ask where you are tempted to perform rather than act. Where do you say the right thing publicly while avoiding the harder private choice? This gap is where integrity erodes quietly.

Learn from leaders who fell not because they lacked intelligence, but because pride and cruelty corroded competence. Pride resists feedback. Cruelty dehumanizes allies and opponents alike. Both shrink perspective. When leaders stop listening and start punishing, they lose information. Decisions worsen. Collapse follows.

Integrity keeps feedback channels open. It invites correction. It accepts accountability without theatrics. This is not humility as posture; it is humility as method.

To make integrity practical, build a personal code. Five non-negotiables you will not betray for convenience. Not slogans—standards. "I do not lie to protect my comfort." "I do not exploit asymmetry of information." "I do not speak with contempt." "I keep promises I make." "I step away when anger clouds judgment." Choose yours carefully. Fewer is better.

Write the code where you can see it. Review it before major decisions. When pressure rises, codes simplify choices. They reduce decision fatigue because the decision was already made. You don't negotiate with yourself in the moment.

Test the code in small ways. Keep a minor promise that would be easy to break. Speak truth gently when silence would be rewarded. Decline an advantage that violates your standard. Each act strengthens the code. Integrity grows through use.

Expect cost. Integrity is not free. It may cost opportunities, approval, or speed. It repays with trust, self-respect, and resilience. Over time, these are compounding assets.

Character is security because it travels with you. When plans fail, character adapts. When praise fades, character steadies. When power tempts, character restrains.

As you finish this chapter, notice where you've been trading integrity for convenience. Bring those trades into the light. Choose differently, once, then again. In the next chapter, you'll learn how to turn character into daily practice—how to build habits and systems that make virtue automatic rather than aspirational.

Chapter 7 — Relationships: The Wisdom of Being Human Together

“If you want to improve, be content to be thought foolish.” — Epictetus

7.1 The Stoic Social Contract: Duty Without Drama

Relationships are where wisdom stops being private and becomes visible. You can hold the clearest principles in solitude and still fail the moment another person enters the room. Stoic thinkers understood this well. They didn’t imagine wisdom as a retreat from human life, but as a way of showing up inside it—steadily, reliably, without unnecessary drama.

The Stoic social contract begins with a simple premise: you are not responsible for controlling others, but you are responsible for playing your role well. Every relationship places you in a role—partner, parent, friend, colleague, neighbor, citizen. These roles are not cages; they are contexts. When you act your part with integrity, friction decreases even when outcomes don’t go your way.

Acting your role well does not mean self-sacrifice or perfection. It means understanding what the role reasonably asks of you and doing that consistently. As a partner, it may mean honesty, presence, and repair after conflict. As a parent, guidance and steadiness rather than emotional reactivity. As a friend, loyalty without possession. As a citizen, participation without contempt. You don't get to choose whether roles exist; you get to choose how you inhabit them.

Most relational suffering comes from role confusion. You expect a friend to meet needs that belong to a partner. You expect a partner to regulate emotions you haven't learned to regulate yourself. You expect colleagues to provide validation instead of collaboration. When expectations drift from roles, disappointment follows. Clarifying roles brings relief.

A useful practice is to ask, in any tense interaction, "What role am I in right now, and what does it ask of me?" This question cuts through ego. It redirects you from being right to being responsible. Responsibility here is not blame; it's authorship. You focus on what you can do next rather than what others failed to do before.

Replace blame with responsibility deliberately. Blame feels powerful, but it immobilizes. It keeps attention fixed on past violations. Responsibility moves attention forward. "What can I contribute now?" is not an admission of fault. It is a declaration of agency. Even when you did nothing wrong, you still have a choice about your next move.

This shift changes the tone of conflict. Instead of rehearsing indictments, you look for repairs. Instead of demanding apologies, you clarify needs. Instead of escalating, you stabilize. The other person may not reciprocate immediately. That's weather. Your contribution remains yours.

Stoic benevolence is central here. Benevolence means wishing others well and acting kindly where possible, without attaching your worth to their response. This is kindness without dependence. You help because it's aligned with who you are, not because you need gratitude or approval.

Approval-hunting corrodes relationships quietly. When kindness is transactional, resentment builds. You give to get. When the return doesn't arrive, you feel used. Benevolence without dependence avoids this trap. You choose kindness freely and release the outcome. If appreciation comes, you accept it. If it doesn't, you remain intact.

Practice this in small ways. Offer help without announcing it. Listen without steering the conversation back to yourself. Do a considerate act and don't track it. This is not invisibility; it's strength. You are not erasing yourself. You are anchoring behavior in values rather than feedback.

Being content to be thought foolish fits here. Improvement often looks awkward from the outside. Choosing patience when sarcasm would win laughs. Asking a clarifying question instead of delivering a clever jab. Admitting uncertainty instead of performing certainty. These choices may cost status in the moment. They build trust over time.

Historically, stable communities depended on this ethic. People understood that harmony was not the absence of conflict, but the presence of shared responsibility. They corrected without humiliation. They disagreed without contempt. They played their parts even when recognition was scarce.

Apply this ethic today by narrowing your focus. In your closest relationship, identify one role-based action you can take this week that would reduce friction. Not a speech. An action. Show up on time. Follow through. Repair quickly. These moves are unglamorous and powerful.

In wider circles, practice civic Stoicism. You may disagree strongly. You may feel unheard. Act your part anyway. Speak truthfully. Vote, participate, volunteer, contribute. Do not let frustration turn into withdrawal or cruelty. Withdrawal abandons the field. Cruelty poisons it.

Duty without drama does not mean suppressing emotion. It means refusing to turn emotion into theater. You can feel hurt and still respond cleanly. You can feel angry and still speak with respect. You can feel disappointed and still keep your word.

As you integrate this section, notice where drama has been substituting for duty. Where intensity has replaced consistency. Where blame has replaced contribution. Shift one interaction. That's enough to begin.

In the next section, you'll learn how to communicate with clarity and generosity—how to speak and listen in ways that reduce misunderstanding and deepen trust without sacrificing honesty.

7.2 Eastern Listening: Presence as Love

Most conflicts don't begin with malice. They begin with not being heard. Eastern traditions place listening at the center of relationship wisdom because listening is where presence becomes tangible. To listen well is not to wait politely for your turn. It is to give another person temporary refuge from being evaluated, corrected, or outperformed.

Begin with empty cup listening. The image is simple: if your cup is full—of opinions, rehearsed replies, judgments—nothing new can enter. Empty cup listening means you hear without preparing your rebuttal. You don't abandon discernment; you postpone it. You let the other person finish their thought without steering it toward your conclusion.

Notice how difficult this is in practice. The moment someone speaks, the mind jumps ahead. It formulates counters. It scans for flaws. It searches for relevance to your own story. Empty cup listening asks you to stay with what is actually being said. The words. The tone. The pauses. The emotion beneath the argument.

A practical way to train this is to summarize before responding. Not theatrically. Simply reflect back what you heard in your own words. "What I'm hearing is that you felt overlooked and frustrated." This does not mean you agree. It means you understand. Understanding calms the nervous system. Calm makes dialogue possible.

Notice ego in conversation. Ego is not always loud. Often it's a quiet itch. The itch to win the point. To sound intelligent. To be admired. To correct. This itch pulls attention away from listening and toward performance. When you notice it, name it internally and return to listening. The itch loses power when it's seen.

Eastern insight treats conversation as a shared field rather than a contest. When you stop trying to win, something surprising happens: truth surfaces more easily. People reveal what actually matters when they don't feel under threat. Your influence increases not because you dominate, but because you create safety.

Silence is an underrated tool here. Many people rush to fill gaps because silence feels awkward. Used skillfully, silence invites depth. When you pause after someone speaks, you signal that you're still with them. Often they continue and say what they really meant. Calm space resolves more than words because it allows insight to arise without force.

Practice using silence intentionally. After a difficult statement, wait a few seconds. Breathe. Maintain eye contact if appropriate. Let the moment settle. This pause prevents reactive replies and often softens the exchange. Silence is not withdrawal; it is containment.

Presence as love means you offer attention without agenda. You don't listen to fix. You don't listen to score points. You listen to understand. This does not mean you avoid hard truths. It means you deliver them from connection rather than contempt.

Apply this in one conversation this week. Choose someone who matters to you. Practice empty cup listening for five minutes. Summarize what you hear. Notice the effect. Most people relax when they feel heard. Some become emotional. This is not your responsibility to manage; it's information about unmet needs finally given room.

Over time, this practice changes your reputation quietly. You become someone people trust with complexity. They bring you real issues, not just polished stories. Relationships deepen because presence is rare and therefore precious.

7.3 Historical Friendship and Counsel

History reminds us that character is shaped in company. The people you keep influence what you tolerate, what you attempt, and what you excuse. Wise individuals were deliberate about counsel. They did not choose companions solely for amusement or affirmation. They chose them for virtue.

Choose mentors and friends by virtue, not entertainment value. Entertainment is easy to find. Virtue is rarer. A virtuous friend is not one who never disagrees, but one who cares more about your growth than your comfort. They celebrate your wins without envy and challenge your blind spots without cruelty.

Ask what qualities you admire in those closest to you. Honesty. Courage. Steadiness. Kindness. If these are absent, ask what is being reinforced instead. Sarcasm. Cynicism. Excess. Avoidance. You become fluent in the emotional language you hear most often.

Build a council of voices deliberately. Not a crowd. A few people who have earned the right to tell you the truth kindly. These are people you consult before major decisions, not after. People who ask hard questions without needing to win. People who will say, "I think you're wrong," and stay with you afterward.

Diversity matters in this council. Not diversity as ornament, but as perspective. Different ages. Different backgrounds. Different temperaments. This prevents echo chambers. When multiple thoughtful people disagree with you in similar ways, pay attention. That's signal.

Conflict is inevitable in any meaningful relationship. How you handle it determines whether trust grows or erodes. Handle conflict like a diplomat. A diplomat protects two things simultaneously: the relationship and the boundary. Lose either and the outcome degrades.

Begin by naming shared interest. “I value our relationship.” Then state the boundary clearly. “This doesn’t work for me.” Avoid character attacks. Focus on behavior and impact. Invite repair without demanding submission. Diplomacy is firm without humiliation.

Historically, durable alliances survived because leaders separated disagreement from disrespect. They argued fiercely without scorning the person. They knew contempt ends cooperation. Even when alliances dissolved, they did so with restraint, preserving future possibility.

Practice diplomatic conflict in low-stakes settings. Express a preference. Decline an invitation. Offer feedback. Each clean exchange builds confidence. You learn that honesty does not destroy connection when delivered with respect.

As you complete this chapter, notice the throughline. Relationships thrive on duty without drama, presence without agenda, and counsel without flattery. These are not tricks. They are disciplines. Practiced daily, they transform how human beings move together.

In the next chapter, you’ll learn how to integrate all of this wisdom into action under uncertainty—how to decide, commit, and adapt without losing your center when outcomes are unclear and stakes are real.

Chapter 8 — Adversity: Turning Trials Into Training

"The impediment to action advances action. What stands in the way becomes the way." — Marcus Aurelius

8.1 Stoic Alchemy: Obstacle → Material

Adversity feels like an interruption. A delay. A detour you didn't agree to. The Stoic move is to see it differently—not as a poetic consolation, but as a practical shift that restores agency. When something blocks your path, it doesn't just stop progress. It offers material. Material for training the exact capacities a good life requires.

This is Stoic alchemy. You don't pretend the obstacle is pleasant. You ask what it can be used for. The question changes your posture immediately. You stop bracing against reality and start working with it.

Begin with a simple reframe: this is practice. Not punishment. Not proof of failure. Practice. When patience is required, the delay becomes the gym. When courage is required, the risk becomes the gym. When discipline is required, the monotony becomes the gym. You don't need to like the workout to benefit from it. You need to show up.

Say it plainly when friction appears: this is practice for patience. Or courage. Or humility. Or endurance. Name the virtue being trained. This naming converts helplessness into purpose. You are no longer waiting for life to resume; you are actively training within it.

Notice how different this feels from forced positivity. You are not saying, “This is good.” You are saying, “This is usable.” Usable experiences restore dignity. They keep you in authorship even when conditions are unfair.

Eastern traditions add an important nuance here. Resistance multiplies suffering. Pain is unavoidable; friction is part of being alive. Suffering grows when you insist that the moment should not be happening. When you accept the moment as it is, without surrendering values, energy frees up. You can act.

This acceptance is not passivity. It’s clarity. You see the obstacle clearly and choose how to respond. The obstacle becomes raw material instead of an enemy.

Negative visualization is the second tool, and it requires care. Used poorly, it feeds anxiety. Used well, it reduces fragility and entitlement. The Stoics practiced it to remind themselves of what they could lose—not to dwell there, but to appreciate what they had and prepare for change.

Practice this briefly and calmly. Imagine a reasonable loss. Not the worst imaginable catastrophe, but something within the realm of possibility. A plan falls apart. A role ends. Health fluctuates. Then ask: what would remain? Which skills, relationships, and inner capacities would still be available?

This exercise does two things. It reduces entitlement—the quiet assumption that things should continue uninterrupted. And it builds resilience. You discover that even if conditions shift, you are not erased. You still have judgment. You still have agency. You still have character.

Entitlement is fragile because it expects life to cooperate. When life doesn't, outrage or despair follows. Preparation replaces entitlement with readiness. You stop demanding guarantees and start strengthening capacity.

Use negative visualization sparingly. Once or twice a week. Keep it short. End by returning attention to the present and appreciating what is currently intact. The goal is not to harden the heart, but to soften surprise.

The third practice is building a response inventory. When adversity hits, decision-making narrows. Stress reduces options. If you haven't preloaded responses, you default to habit—often the least skillful one. A response inventory gives you ready moves when clarity is scarce.

Think back to past challenges. What helped? Breathing before reacting. Calling a specific person. Writing to clarify. Physical movement. Stepping away for twenty-four hours before deciding. These are not generic tips; they are your proven tools. Inventory them.

Write them down mentally or on paper. "When overwhelmed, I walk for ten minutes." "When angry, I delay sending messages overnight." "When discouraged, I return to fundamentals." This is not rigidity; it's preparation. Athletes rehearse responses so they don't freeze under pressure. You can too.

Add one new response deliberately. Something you want to practice using when the next obstacle arrives. Keep it simple and repeatable. The inventory grows over time. With it, adversity becomes less chaotic. You know what to do first.

History shows this pattern repeatedly. Those who endured repeated trials were not superhuman. They were prepared. They had routines, principles, and fallback moves. When plans failed, they executed the basics. When pressure rose, they returned to what they had practiced.

This is why adversity reveals character rather than creating it. Under stress, you don't rise to the occasion; you fall to your level of preparation. Stoic alchemy is about raising that level before the test.

As you practice this approach, notice a subtle shift. You stop asking, "Why is this happening to me?" and start asking, "What is this training me for?" The second question restores momentum. You may not know the final answer yet. You don't need to. Training works even when the future is unclear.

This mindset also changes how you view others under strain. You see their behavior as untrained or overwhelmed rather than malicious. This doesn't excuse harm, but it tempers your response. You protect boundaries without contempt.

Adversity, then, becomes a teacher that doesn't require your admiration. It requires your attention. You learn by doing, by responding, by refining. Each obstacle adds a layer of competence if you let it.

As you move forward, carry this lens lightly. Not everything needs to be reframed immediately. Some moments require grief or rest first. Alchemy is patient. When you're ready, you return to the question of use.

In the next section, you'll learn how to endure prolonged difficulty without hardening—how to sustain effort, hope, and meaning when trials are not brief but extended.

8.2 Eastern Resilience: Non-Resistance, Not Passivity

Resilience is often confused with toughness—clenching teeth and pushing through at any cost. Eastern traditions offer a quieter, more durable version. Resilience is non-resistance to reality paired with wise action within it. You accept what is happening without surrendering your ability to respond. Acceptance is clarity. Surrender is abdication. The difference matters.

Acceptance says, "This is the situation." It stops the internal argument. It ends the exhausting negotiation with facts. Surrender says, "There is nothing to be done." It drains initiative. When you accept without surrender, energy returns because you're no longer spending it on denial. You can place it where it counts.

Practice this distinction deliberately. When adversity hits, name the facts without commentary. What has actually happened? What has changed? What remains intact? Keep the language plain. Avoid adjectives that smuggle judgment. This grounding step steadies the nervous system. From steadiness, action becomes possible.

The next move is to let go of the second arrow. In Eastern teaching, the first arrow is the unavoidable pain of an event. The second arrow is the mental suffering you add—stories about injustice, permanence, or personal failure. The first arrow hurts. The second multiplies pain.

Notice the second arrow in real time. It sounds like "This always happens to me," or "I won't recover," or "This means I'm weak."

These statements are not facts; they are interpretations delivered with conviction. You don't need to silence them. You need to see them. Label them as stories and return to the present task.

Letting go of the second arrow does not minimize loss. It prevents compounding it. You allow grief, fear, or frustration to move through without layering shame or catastrophe on top. This is emotional efficiency. You conserve strength for what actually helps.

Under stress, complexity becomes a liability. Simplicity is a form of care. Reduce commitments. Narrow priorities. Decide what must be done today and what can wait. This is not giving up; it's triage. You stabilize the system before expanding again.

Create a short list of non-negotiables during hard periods. Sleep enough to function. Eat simply. Move your body a little. Keep one meaningful connection alive. Everything else is optional. This simplification lowers cognitive load and preserves morale.

Eastern resilience trusts that clarity emerges when noise is reduced. You don't need to solve everything now. You need to keep the essentials intact. From there, the next step reveals itself.

8.3 Historical Endurance: What Keeps People Standing

History shows that endurance is not sustained by willpower alone. Those who lasted through prolonged hardship relied on a triad: meaning, community, and routine. Remove one and the structure weakens. Remove two and collapse accelerates.

Meaning answers the question, "Why continue?" It does not need to be grand. It needs to be true. Caring for someone. Completing a responsibility. Preserving dignity. Meaning turns suffering from pointless to purposeful. Without meaning, effort feels punitive.

Community provides witness and support. Humans are not designed to endure alone. Even a small circle matters. One person who checks in. One shared meal. One honest conversation. Community does not fix everything, but it distributes the load.

Routine is the unsung hero. Routine carries you when motivation fails. Simple, repeatable actions anchor days that would otherwise blur. Wake at a consistent time. Eat at regular hours. Walk the same route. Write a few lines. Routine restores predictability when the world is unstable.

Build hardship rituals deliberately. Sleep becomes sacred. Protect it. Movement becomes medicine. Keep it gentle and consistent. Journaling becomes a pressure valve. Write what happened, what you feel, and what you will do next. Deliberate calm—breathing, quiet sitting—keeps the nervous system from spiraling.

Avoid the hero narrative. Dramatic endurance looks impressive and burns out fast. Steady endurance looks ordinary and lasts. You don't need to prove strength. You need to preserve it. History remembers those who kept going, not those who flamed out brightly.

Steady means showing up again tomorrow. It means choosing rest over theatrics. It means asking for help without shame. It means adjusting expectations without abandoning standards.

As you integrate these practices, notice how adversity changes shape. It remains difficult, but it becomes navigable. You stop measuring yourself by intensity and start measuring by continuity.

In the next chapter, you'll learn how to decide and act when the path is unclear—how to commit without guarantees and adapt without losing direction.

Chapter 9 — Power, Freedom, and the Self: Not Becoming Your Own Tyrant

"No man is free who is not master of himself." — often attributed to Epictetus

9.1 Internal Freedom: The Sovereignty of Choice

Power is usually imagined as something external—status, money, authority, influence over others. Freedom is imagined as the absence of constraint. Both ideas miss the deeper battlefield. The most consequential power you will ever wield is the power over your own choices in ordinary moments. Lose that, and no amount of external freedom compensates. Keep it, and even constrained circumstances remain livable.

Internal freedom is sovereignty of choice. It is the capacity to decide rather than react. To pause rather than compulsively obey the first impulse that appears. This sovereignty is not a personality trait. It is a trained condition. And like any sovereignty, it can be eroded quietly from within.

Start by noticing compulsions. Not dramatic addictions necessarily, but the small, frequent behaviors that bypass choice. Scrolling when bored. Reaching for sugar when tired. Seeking approval when uncertain. Consuming outrage when restless. These are not moral failures. They are signals that something inside you is being governed automatically.

Compulsion feels like relief in the moment and regret afterward. You do it quickly, almost invisibly, and only later notice the cost—lost time, dulled focus, agitation, dependence. Each compulsion slightly weakens the sense that you are choosing your life. Over time, they add up to a subtle tyranny: you are busy, stimulated, and strangely less free.

The Stoics did not try to eliminate desire. They trained consent. They asked whether an impulse deserved obedience. This question alone restores dignity. You move from being pushed to choosing.

Begin with awareness without condemnation. Track one compulsion for a week. Just one. Notice when it appears, what precedes it, and what follows it. Boredom. Fatigue. Social anxiety. Uncertainty. Compulsions are rarely random. They are attempts to regulate internal states quickly.

Once you see the pattern, introduce friction. Freedom grows when bad habits are harder and good habits are easier. Willpower is unreliable; environment is dependable. Friction is not punishment. It is design.

Make the compulsion slightly inconvenient. Log out. Delete the app from the home screen. Keep sweets out of immediate reach. Turn off notifications that provoke outrage. Add a step that requires intention. When there is a pause, choice can re-enter.

At the same time, remove friction from behaviors you want to strengthen. Place the book where the phone used to be. Prepare healthy food in advance. Keep workout clothes visible. Set reminders for the practices you value. This is not self-control through force. It is self-leadership through structure.

Eastern traditions emphasize that craving weakens when it is not constantly indulged. You don't fight the urge; you let it crest and fall. Friction creates the space for this to happen. The urge arrives, you notice it, and because action is not immediate, it passes. Each time you allow this cycle to complete, tolerance increases.

Train discomfort tolerance deliberately. Freedom grows where avoidance shrinks. Avoidance teaches the nervous system that discomfort is dangerous. Tolerance teaches it that discomfort is survivable. You don't need extreme practices. Small, chosen discomfort is enough.

Sit with boredom for two minutes without reaching for stimulation. Delay a response when you want reassurance. Choose a simpler meal. Walk when you'd rather scroll. These acts are not about suffering; they are about proving to yourself that you can feel discomfort without collapsing or compensating.

Discomfort tolerance restores optionality. When you are no longer compelled to escape every unpleasant sensation, you can choose actions based on values rather than relief. You stop being governed by the shortest path to comfort.

Historical examples make this clear. Those who lost internal freedom often did so during periods of ease. Excess softened resistance. Small indulgences accumulated into dependence. When conditions changed, they lacked the discipline to adapt.

Those who maintained internal freedom practiced restraint when it was unnecessary so it was available when it mattered.

There is a paradox here. Discipline increases freedom. Not the discipline of rigidity, but the discipline of choice. Each time you choose deliberately, you reinforce sovereignty. Each time you obey compulsion, you outsource it.

Watch how approval operates as a compulsion. The urge to be liked can steer decisions quietly. You say yes when you mean no. You soften truths. You perform. Approval feels safe, but it's volatile. It hands power to others' reactions. Internal freedom requires that you act from standards, not applause.

Outrage is another compulsion masquerading as righteousness. It offers instant energy and moral clarity. It also consumes attention and narrows thinking. Notice when outrage pulls you into cycles that don't improve your life or the world. Step back. Choose engagement where it produces results, not just stimulation.

None of this requires becoming austere or joyless. Joy chosen freely is richer than pleasure taken compulsively. When you are not driven, enjoyment deepens. You savor rather than binge. You rest rather than numb.

A simple daily practice strengthens sovereignty. At the end of the day, recall one moment when you chose deliberately and one when you acted on impulse. No judgment. Just noticing. This reflection builds awareness, and awareness precedes change.

Internal freedom is quiet. It doesn't announce itself. It shows up as steadiness. As fewer regrets. As mornings that begin with intention rather than urgency. Over time, it changes how power feels. You stop trying to dominate circumstances and start governing yourself.

This is the freedom no one can take from you—and the one you can give away incrementally if you're not attentive. In the next section, you'll learn how to handle external power—status, authority, influence—without letting it distort your character or turn you into the very tyrant you once resisted.

9.2 Eastern Selfhood: Identity as a Useful Fiction

Power over yourself weakens when identity hardens. Eastern traditions approach identity with a surprising gentleness: the self is treated not as a fixed object to defend, but as a useful fiction—a story that helps you function, coordinate, and make meaning. Trouble begins when the story is mistaken for the truth.

Notice the "I-story" running quietly in the background. "I'm the responsible one." "I'm bad at conflict." "I'm the kind of person who never quits." These stories feel stabilizing. They also narrow possibility. When identity hardens, choices shrink. You stop asking what's wise now and start asking what fits the story. Suffering follows because reality keeps changing while the story resists updating.

Observe how identity creates pressure. When you say, "I am this," you also say, "I cannot be that." The mind then works to protect consistency, even when it costs you growth or peace. You defend habits that no longer serve you. You reject opportunities that threaten the story. You cling to roles long after they've expired.

Eastern practice invites observation rather than rebellion. You don't need to destroy identity. You need to see it. When a strong self-statement arises, add a soft qualifier: "I'm telling myself the story that…" This creates space. The story remains usable without being tyrannical. You regain choice.

Flexibility is the next skill. You are allowed to change your mind. You are allowed to revise your life. This sounds obvious and feels transgressive because many identities are built on consistency for its own sake. Consistency is useful when it aligns with values. It is harmful when it becomes a cage.

Practice flexibility in small ways. Admit uncertainty where you once performed certainty. Try a new approach to a familiar problem. Update an opinion with new evidence. Each act weakens the illusion that the self must remain static. You become responsive rather than rigid.

Beginner mind is the antidote to cynicism and arrogance. Cynicism says, "I've seen this before; it won't work." Arrogance says, "I already know." Beginner mind says, "Let's see." It doesn't deny experience; it refuses to be imprisoned by it.

Adopt beginner mind intentionally. Enter conversations curious rather than armed. Approach skills as learnable rather than settled. Treat people as unfolding rather than finished. This posture restores vitality. It also protects freedom because you are no longer bound to defend a reputation of knowing.

When identity loosens, compassion increases—toward yourself and others. You stop demanding that life confirm who you think you are. You allow yourself to evolve. Freedom expands because choice is no longer filtered through a brittle self-image.

9.3 Historical Power: The Corruption Test

External power amplifies whatever is already present. History is unambiguous here. Power does not create character; it reveals it. Under low accountability, tendencies become behaviors. This is the corruption test.

Ask yourself a sobering question: if you had more power tomorrow, would you become better or louder? Better means more patient, more fair, more restrained. Louder means more entitled, more reactive, more convinced of your own correctness. The answer is not fixed. It depends on the habits you're training now.

Study incentives wherever power appears. When rewards are immediate and consequences are delayed, distortion grows. When praise is abundant and feedback is scarce, blind spots widen. Power reveals character under these conditions because self-regulation becomes optional.

Build self-checks before you need them. Advisors who can disagree with you without fear. Rules you follow even when you could bend them. Transparency where secrecy would be easier. These checks are not signs of weakness. They are signs of foresight.

Historically, the most durable leaders constrained themselves. They invited counsel. They set limits. They ritualized humility. Those who didn't drifted. First subtly, then decisively. The fall rarely came from one large abuse. It came from many small permissions granted to the ego.

Create humility practices. Regularly seek criticism from someone you respect. Rotate roles where you are not in charge. Engage in work that offers no applause. These practices keep power from becoming identity.

Freedom from tyranny—external or internal—requires vigilance. You watch the self as closely as you watch circumstances. You question stories. You design checks. You choose growth over volume.

As you close this chapter, remember the central paradox: mastery of self increases freedom, while unchecked power—over habits, identity, or others—shrinks it. In the final chapter, you will bring all of this together into a living practice: how to carry wisdom forward daily, without rigidity, and keep becoming more free over time.

Chapter 10 — Meaning and the Deep Life: A Personal Philosophy You Can Live

"The unexamined life is not worth living." — Socrates

10.1 Your North Star: Values That Survive Seasons

Meaning is not something you discover once and then possess. It is something you practice. It survives seasons because it is built from values that can move with you—through success and failure, through expansion and contraction, through certainty and doubt. When meaning collapses, it's rarely because life became hard. It's because the philosophy guiding your days was borrowed, vague, or outpaced by change.

A personal philosophy you can live begins with values that are active. Not adjectives you admire, but verbs you practice. Verbs move. Verbs adapt. Verbs survive seasons.

Start by defining five core values as verbs. Five is enough to be comprehensive without becoming diluted. Fewer than five can become brittle; more than five become decorative. Choose verbs that describe how you want to move through the world, not how you want to appear within it.

Examples help, but they are not templates. "Create" points toward making, shaping, expressing. "Serve" points toward contribution and usefulness. “Learn” points toward growth and humility. “Protect” points toward stewardship—of people, time, health, or principles. “Simplify” points toward restraint and clarity. These verbs are durable because they can be enacted in many forms.

Your verbs should pass a simple test: can you practice them on a difficult day? If a value requires ideal conditions, it will fail you when you need it most. “Be happy” collapses under pressure. “Show up” does not. “Be successful” depends on outcomes. “Practice excellence” depends on effort.

Write your five verbs and define them in your own words. One sentence each. Keep the language plain. This is not branding. It’s instruction. “Create means I bring something into the world regularly, even when imperfect.” “Serve means I leave people and places better than I found them.” “Learn means I update beliefs with evidence.” Definitions turn inspiration into behavior.

Next, test your values against time. Ask whether each verb would still matter if circumstances changed dramatically. If your role ended. If recognition disappeared. If resources tightened. Values that survive these tests are likely to survive seasons. Values that don’t may be aspirations masquerading as anchors.

Once values are defined, alignment becomes the real work. Alignment is where philosophy meets reality. It answers a sobering question: does your schedule reflect what you say matters? Because your schedule is your real philosophy. Not your intentions. Not your explanations. Your calendar and your energy allocation reveal what you actually value.

Look at a typical week. Where does time go? Where does attention go? Where does emotional energy go? You don't need to judge this. You need to see it. If "learn" is a core value but there is no protected time for reading, reflection, or skill-building, the value is aspirational, not operational. If "serve" matters but your week has no space for contribution beyond obligation, the value is underfed.

Alignment does not require dramatic overhauls. It requires deliberate rebalancing. Add one block of time that clearly expresses a value. Remove one block that clearly doesn't. This is philosophy enacted. Over time, small adjustments accumulate into a life that feels coherent.

Notice how misalignment feels in the body. Restless. Irritable. Numb. Notice how alignment feels. Quietly satisfying. Grounded. Energizing in a clean way. Use these sensations as feedback. Meaning is not abstract; it is felt.

Values also guide trade-offs. When two good options compete, values decide without drama. You don't ask which is more impressive. You ask which expresses your verbs more fully right now. This reduces regret because the choice is rooted in principle rather than impulse.

To protect meaning, you need boundaries. This is where the yes list and the no list come in. Most people focus only on a to-do list and wonder why life feels crowded and thin. Meaning requires exclusion.

Your yes list is a short set of commitments that directly express your values. Not tasks, but categories. "Weekly creative work."

"Daily movement." "Regular time with family." "Monthly learning project." These are non-negotiables. They go on the calendar first.

Your no list is just as important. It names what you refuse because it erodes alignment. "No meetings without an agenda." "No commitments made from guilt." "No scrolling before noon." "No work that violates my standards." The no list protects the yes list. Without it, values are constantly outbid by convenience.

Creating a no list can feel uncomfortable because it reveals where you've been trading meaning for ease or approval. That discomfort is instructive. It points to places where boundaries will restore energy.

Historically, people who lived deeply were selective. Not busy. Selective. They chose a narrow set of commitments and honored them over time. They said no early and often so they could say yes fully. This was not selfishness. It was stewardship of attention.

Eastern insight adds another layer. Values should guide action without becoming another identity to defend. You practice values; you don't perform them. When values become performance, they stiffen. When practiced quietly, they stay alive.

Allow values to evolve. Not every year. Not impulsively. But as seasons change. What "serve" looks like at one stage may differ at another. The verb remains; the expression updates. This flexibility keeps philosophy relevant rather than nostalgic.

A useful weekly reflection reinforces alignment. Ask three questions. Where did I live my values this week? Where did I drift? What one adjustment would bring me closer next week? This is not moral accounting. It's course correction.

Meaning is not found by asking, "What is the purpose of life?" It's built by asking, "What is my next right action, guided by values I trust?" Over time, these actions weave a life that feels intentional even when outcomes are uncertain.

As you work with this section, don't rush to perfect your values. Start them. Use them. Let life test them. Revise with humility. A philosophy you can live is not flawless. It is practiced.

In the next section, you will learn how to turn these values into a simple, durable system—how to review, reset, and recommit so meaning stays active not just in reflection, but in motion.

10.2 Practice as Proof: Daily Rituals of Wisdom

Meaning survives contact with life only when it is practiced. Without practice, philosophy becomes a mood—something you admire when conditions are calm and abandon when pressure rises. Daily rituals turn wisdom into muscle memory. They don't add weight to your schedule; they add coherence to your day.

Begin in the morning with intention, not a to-do list. Before the day starts asking for things, decide who you will be. This takes less than a minute. Choose one quality you want to embody today—patient, honest, focused, generous, courageous. Say it plainly. "Today I will be patient." This is not a wish. It is a standard.

Intention works because it primes attention. When the first irritation arrives, your mind recognizes it as a test rather than a surprise. You don't need to win every test. You need to recognize them. Recognition alone improves behavior. Over time, intention trains identity quietly. You stop asking, "What should I do?" and start asking, "How would someone patient act right now?"

If you want to anchor intention more firmly, pair it with a cue. The first sip of coffee. The moment you sit at your desk. The opening of your door. Let that cue trigger the intention. Repetition links the two. Soon, the quality you chose shows up automatically when the cue appears.

Midday is where meaning often thins. Energy dips. Distractions multiply. This is why a reset matters. Keep it simple: breath plus one courageous act. The breath resets physiology. The act resets agency.

Take ten slow breaths. Longer exhale than inhale. Feel your feet. Name the present moment. Then choose one small act that requires courage. Courage does not have to be public or dramatic. It can be sending a clear message you've been avoiding. Asking for clarification instead of assuming. Stopping a task that isn't aligned. Beginning the one that is.

This midpoint ritual prevents drift. Drift is how good intentions decay. The reset does not demand perfection; it restores direction. You remind yourself that the day is still yours to shape.

Evening is for review, not judgment. Review means looking clearly and kindly. Judgment means punishing yourself for being human. The Stoics were explicit about this distinction. Improvement requires honesty without cruelty.

Ask three questions. What did I do well today? Name specifics. This trains recognition of progress, which sustains effort. What did I do poorly or avoid? Name it without explanation. Explanations protect ego; naming creates leverage. What will I correct tomorrow? Choose one adjustment. Not a reinvention. A correction.

End the review deliberately. Close the notebook. Take a breath. Let the day be complete. This closure matters. It prevents rumination from bleeding into rest. Rest is part of wisdom, not a reward for it.

These rituals are intentionally modest. They survive travel, stress, and change. You can do them anywhere. That is the point. A practice that requires ideal conditions will not last. A practice that fits real life becomes real wisdom.

10.3 The Codex You Leave Behind

A codex is not a book you finish; it's a reference you return to. The final task is to create your personal Wisdom Codex—a living document that distills what you've learned into guidance you can use when clarity is scarce.

Begin by assembling three sets of twenty. Twenty principles. Twenty practices. Twenty reminders. Principles are truths you trust. Practices are actions you repeat. Reminders are phrases that reorient you when you're lost.

Principles might sound like, "I can control my response, not outcomes," or "Discomfort is information, not danger." Practices might be, "Delay messages when angry," or "Walk daily without a phone." Reminders might be, "Slow is smooth," or "Choose dignity over speed." The exact content matters less than ownership. Use your language. Borrow nothing you haven't tested.

This codex should be concise and accessible. One or two pages. Something you can read in five minutes. Keep it where you can find it. Return to it quarterly. Update it as you learn. Wisdom that cannot be updated becomes dogma.

Living historically means acting as an ancestor, not a consumer. Consumers ask what they can get. Ancestors ask what they will leave. This shift changes behavior immediately. You think longer. You choose more carefully. You invest in things that outlast mood.

Ask yourself what you are modeling for those who come after you—children, students, colleagues, strangers who watch how you move through the world. Are you modeling panic or steadiness? Contempt or respect? Depth or distraction? You don't need an audience to act as an ancestor. You need perspective.

History remembers people less for what they owned than for how they treated time, power, and others. It remembers their standards under pressure. Their restraint in abundance. Their generosity when it cost something. These are choices available to you daily.

Make depth visible in quiet ways. Fewer boasts. More craft. More presence. More love. Craft shows in the care you bring to ordinary tasks. Presence shows in how you listen without checking out. Love shows in reliability—doing what you said you would do, especially when it's inconvenient.

Depth does not announce itself. It accumulates. People feel it around you before they can name it. They trust you with more because you've proven consistent. This is legacy in motion.

As you close this book, resist the urge to summarize everything. You don't need to remember all of it. You need to practice a few things well. Choose what resonated. Build it into your days. Let the rest return when needed.

The deepest life is not dramatic. It is deliberate. It is built from small choices made with clarity and repeated with care. You don't need a perfect philosophy. You need a lived one.

Return to your intention tomorrow morning. Take the breath at midday. Review without shame at night. Keep your codex close. Live as if your life is worth studying—because it is.

Conclusion — The Codex Is Not Knowledge, It's Training

"Knowing is not enough; we must apply." — commonly attributed to Goethe

If there is one sentence that belongs at the end of this journey, it is that one. Not because it is clever, but because it is mercilessly true. Knowing is comfortable. Application is costly. Knowing lets you feel aligned without being tested. Application introduces friction, uncertainty, and the quiet exposure of who you are when things don't go your way. This codex was never meant to make you smarter in theory. It was meant to make you steadier in practice.

Across Stoic, Eastern, and historical traditions, wisdom converges on the same conclusion: your life becomes what you repeatedly choose. Not what you intend. Not what you admire. Not what you promise yourself you'll do "someday." What you choose again and again—especially when tired, distracted, or emotional—shapes your character, your relationships, and your sense of meaning.

This is why the codex is not knowledge. It is training. Training assumes imperfection. Training expects missed reps. Training improves through return, not through flawless execution. When you miss a day, you don't quit training. You show up the next day and continue. That mindset alone changes how you live.

Think back over what you've read. Notice which ideas stirred resistance rather than agreement. Those are often the ones you need most. Wisdom doesn't always feel affirming at first; sometimes it feels inconvenient. That inconvenience is a sign you've found an edge worth working.

Before you close this book and place it on a shelf, pause and complete a simple closing protocol. Not as a checklist, but as a commitment to motion.

First, choose three principles you needed most from the book. Not the ones that sounded best. The ones that met you where you actually are. Maybe it's the idea that you control your response, not outcomes. Maybe it's the reminder that fear is a prediction, not a prophecy. Maybe it's the insistence that character is the only real security. Write these principles in your own words. Ownership begins with translation.

These principles are not slogans. They are lenses. You will look through them when stress rises. If you choose too many, you will use none. Three is enough to shape behavior without overwhelming attention.

Next, choose three practices you will do for the next thirty days. Not forever. Thirty days is long enough to feel resistance and short enough to commit honestly. Choose practices that fit your real life, not an idealized version of it.

One might be a morning intention where you decide who you will be before the day decides for you. Another might be a midday reset—breath and one courageous act—so drift doesn't claim the afternoon. A third might be an evening review where you look clearly without shame and adjust gently for tomorrow. Or perhaps your practices come from elsewhere in the book:

voluntary simplicity, one-tasking, friction for compulsions, diplomatic conflict, or a weekly memento mori reflection.

The test is simple. Can you do these practices on a difficult day? If the answer is no, simplify them until the answer becomes yes. Consistency beats intensity every time.

Then choose one relationship you will improve through steadier presence. Just one. Not a campaign to fix everything. A decision to show up more cleanly in one human connection.

This might mean listening without rehearsing your response. It might mean expressing a boundary calmly instead of letting resentment accumulate. It might mean offering reliability instead of grand gestures. Relationships don't deepen through declarations; they deepen through repeated, trustworthy behavior.

Decide what steadier presence looks like in that relationship and practice it for thirty days. Don't announce it. Don't demand reciprocation. Let your behavior do the speaking. Presence, given freely, changes the field more than arguments ever will.

As you move forward, remember this: wisdom does not remove difficulty from life. It removes confusion. Difficulty with clarity is workable. Difficulty with confusion is exhausting. The aim of this codex has been to help you meet reality with fewer distortions, less reactivity, and more choice.

There will be days when you forget everything you've read. That's not failure. That's being human. What matters is whether you remember enough to pause, to choose one clean action, and to begin again. Return is the skill. Return is the practice.

You don't need to become a different person to live a deeper life. You need to become more deliberate about the person you already are. You need to notice what you do under pressure and train there. You need to decide what you stand for before the moment demands it.

The deepest life is not louder. It doesn't perform wisdom. It lives it quietly. It is clearer because it sees what matters. Kinder because it understands what drives people. More intentional because it refuses to drift unconsciously.

If you do the small things this codex asks—choose principles, practice daily, show up steadily in one relationship—you will not just understand wisdom. You will embody it. And over time, without fanfare, you will notice something profound: your life will feel less chaotic, less reactive, and more your own.

That is the promise of training. Not mastery. Ownership. Not perfection. Direction. Not noise. Depth.

Close the book. Open the day. Practice.

www.ingramcontent.com/pod-product-compliance
Lightning Source LLC
LaVergne TN
LVHW020649100826
845148LV00012B/2390